IN A PERFECT WORLD

The War on

Hunger

Dealing with Dictators,

Deserts,

and Debt

Ron Fridell

Twenty-First Century Books / Brookfield, Connecticut

Cover photograph courtesy of © WFP/Alejandro Chicheri; © IDE; © Gamma Presse/Thomas White

Photographs courtesy of Peter Arnold, Inc. (© Still Pictures): p. 1; Woodfin Camp & Associates: pp. 13 (© Betty Press), 35 (© Betty Press), 38 (bottom © Mike Yamashita); Magnum Photos: pp. 14 (© C. Steele-Perkins), 30 (© P. J. Griffiths); Corbis: pp. 23 (© Stephanie Maze), 24 (© Reuters NewMedia, Inc.), 48 (© AFP), 57 (© Robert Maass), 67 (© Abbie Enick/Travel Ink); Heifer International: pp. 26, 27; Peter Arnold, Inc.: pp. 32 (© Still Pictures), 38 (top © Still Pictures); IDE: p. 36; WFP/Alejandro Chicheri: p. 54; Photo Edit, Inc.: pp. 60 (© Tony Freeman), 71 (© David Young-Wolff); Gamma Presse Images: p. 63 (© Michael Sofronski)

Maps by Mary Ellen Casey

Library of Congress Cataloging-in-Publication Data
Fridell, Ron.
The war on hunger : dealing with dictators, deserts, and debt / Ron Fridell.
p. cm.—(In a perfect world)
Includes bibliographical references and index.
ISBN 0-7613-2650-2 (lib. bdg.)
1. Food relief—Juvenile literature.   2. Food supply—Juvenile literature.
3. Hunger—Juvenile literature.   4. Malnutrition—Juvenile literature.
[1. Hunger. 2. Food supply. 3. Food relief.] I. Title. II. Series.
HV696.F6 F75 2003
363.8'83—dc21
2002005059

Published by Twenty-First Century Books
A Division of The Millbrook Press, Inc.
2 Old New Milford Road
Brookfield, Connecticut 06804
http://www.millbrookpress.com

Contents

Introduction
Serious
Hunger

Some people know only one kind of hunger: the mild dis comfort they feel shortly before a meal. Sometimes they say things like, "When do we eat? I'm starving!"

They're not really starving, of course. They're not seri ously hungry. About the longest they ever go without a satis fying meal is twelve hours. This brief and mild discomfort is what they know as hunger.

This book is not about that kind of hunger. This book is about the serious kind of hunger that lasts for weeks, months, years.

Chapter 1

800 Million Short of Perfect

Mumba Mwansa lives in Zambia, in southern Africa. He is seven years old. On good days, Mumba eats three meals. In the morning he has boiled sweet potato and roasted groundnuts. In the afternoon he eats cassava, a root vegetable similar to potatoes, and some fish. At night he has more cassava along with a bit of fish.

On bad days, Mumba has only one small meal. But even on good days, Mumba does not get enough of the right kinds of foods to eat. His diet is low in fat, iron, and calcium, three ingredients his body must have to grow up healthy. On average, he gets only about two-thirds of the nourishment his body needs. Many of the children in the area where Mumba lives do not get enough of the right kinds of foods to grow up strong and healthy.[1]

Hungry People

In a perfect world all people would have enough good, nutritious food to eat well every day of their lives. At the present time, though, some 800 million people worldwide suffer the harsh effects of serious, long-lasting hunger.[2] That's about one of every eight people on Earth. This is 100 million people more than the populations of the United States, Canada, and Western Europe combined. Most of these 800 million seriously hungry people get just enough to eat to keep them from starving, but they don't get enough nutritious food to keep them healthy.

The energy supplied by the food that people eat is measured in units called calories. The average child of seven needs about 1,800 calories a day to stay healthy.[3] The average adult needs about 2,500 calories.[4] Seriously hungry people do not get enough to eat on a daily basis to meet this minimum need.

Most hungry people have some cereal grains to eat—rice, corn, and wheat. They often make the grains into flour and then cook the flour into a form of bread or pasta. Grain gives seriously hungry people some of the nutrients their bodies need, but they don't always get enough grain. And they seldom get enough milk, meat, fish, or fresh fruits or vegetables to supply the rest of the nutrients their bodies require.

When a person suffers serious hunger for more than a few days, the body starts consuming reserves of stored fat to make up the difference. A healthy person's body can afford to lose about 30 percent of its weight. But once this fat is burned away, the body begins consuming vital proteins in muscles and organs. Then a person's health is at risk.

Malnutrition and Children

Every year millions of people die because of hunger. Most casualties of hunger don't die from starvation, though. They die from the accumulated effects of long-lasting hunger, which is known as *malnutrition*. Malnutrition weakens the body's ability to ward off disease. The immune system breaks down, and the body loses its ability to fight infection. Then, without proper medical treatment, even a fairly mild health problem, such as diarrhea or respiratory infection, can be fatal.

Nurta Abdulkadir has seen the terrifying effects of malnutrition. She works for the United Nations (UN), an organization of world leaders dedicated to establishing peace and security in the world. Ms. Abdulkadir is a health and nutrition worker in the north African country of Somalia. She has helped people who must survive on shriveled fruits and handfuls of leaves. She speaks of a mother who has seen two of her six children die in one month: "The mother told me it was from lack of food," Ms. Abdulkadir says, "but of course exhaustion, malaria and repeated bouts of diarrhea are also critical causes."[5]

An estimated 183 million children suffer from malnutrition.[6] The effects of malnutrition are both physically and mentally hard on children. A child's body needs a steady supply of nourishment to keep growing. The body of a malnourished child will be stunted, or kept from growing to full size. A person suffering from stunted growth will be weaker and less healthy than a person who has grown to full, natural size.

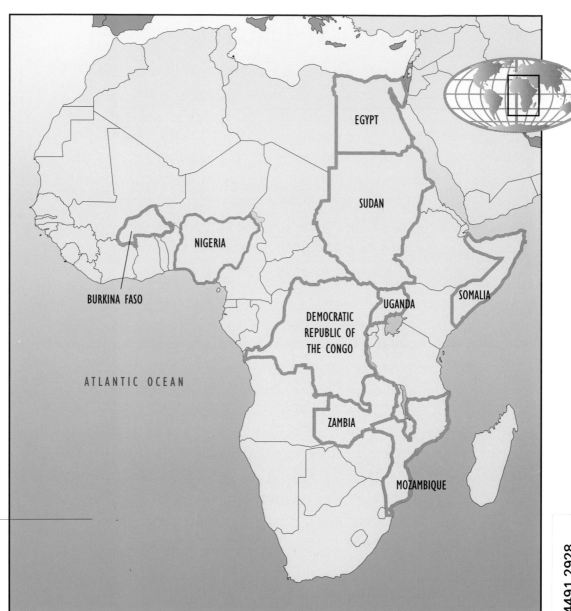

EGYPT

SUDAN

NIGERIA

BURKINA FASO

DEMOCRATIC
REPUBLIC OF
THE CONGO

UGANDA

SOMALIA

ATLANTIC OCEAN

ZAMBIA

MOZAMBIQUE

*Many countries in Africa are the focus of
the war on hunger. Some of the countries
discussed in this book are highlighted here.*

Severe malnutrition can lead to a disease known as kwashiorkor (KWA·she·OR·kor), which causes the body's tissues to swell, making the victim look overweight. Many malnourished children suffer from kwashiorkor. The death rate from this protein-deficiency disease is 80 percent.

A child's mental capacity also suffers when nourishment is lacking. A healthy brain grows faster than the rest of the body. By age four, a child's brain has already grown to 90 percent of its adult weight, compared with 20 percent for the rest of the body. The brain of a malnourished child will be stunted. This loss of size results in a lower-than-normal level of intelligence that can never be made up.

Hungry Societies

Besides harming people, serious hunger can cripple entire societies. Hunger makes people restless and angry. It leads to crime and political unrest. It fuels revolution, terrorism, and war. Hunger makes people depressed. It dulls their minds and senses, and they have a hard time paying attention. Hungry children can't learn in school, and hungry adults can't be productive at their jobs. When people can't be productive, their entire society suffers.

A Need for Action

World leaders have been aware of the problem of world hunger for many years. At a 1974 UN conference on food, world leaders declared:

Every man, woman and child has the inalienable right to be free from hunger and malnutrition in order to develop fully and maintain their physical and mental faculties. Society today already possesses sufficient resources, organizational ability and technology and hence the competence to achieve this objective.[7]

But these world leaders did not propose an action plan for ending world hunger.

At another UN conference on food in 1996, world leaders again addressed the problem of world hunger. They declared that the number of hungry people in the world would be reduced to 400 million by no later than 2015. But once again, world leaders did not propose an action plan for achieving their goal.

Waging the War on Hunger

Despite this lack of action, the number of seriously hungry people has been declining, from about 1 billion in 1970 to about 800 million in 2000. The number continues to decline at the rate of about 6 million per year.[8] But in some parts of the developing world, including most of the continent of Africa, the number of seriously hungry people is rising, not falling.

The branch of the UN that deals with world hunger is the Food and Agricultural Organization (FAO). In May 2001, the FAO director-general, Dr. Jacques Diouf, called for a stepped-up war on hunger. Dr. Diouf warned: "Unless efforts are stepped up by national governments, international bodies, and organizations of the civil society, widespread hunger . . . will remain with us in the decades to come."[9]

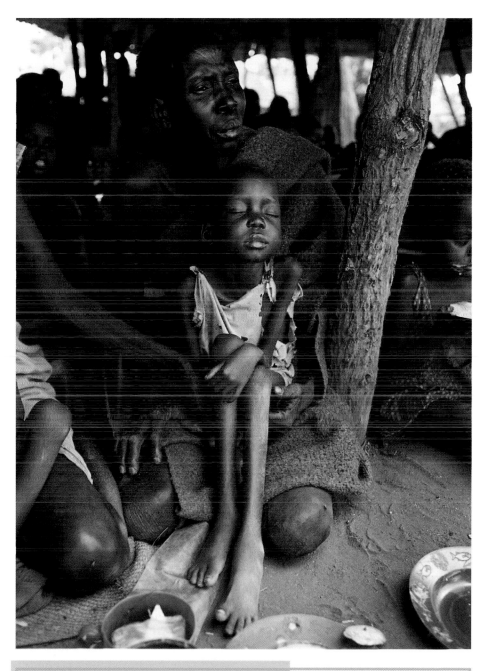

This child from Sudan in Africa suffers from severe hunger and malnutrition. This kind of condition often leads to serious health problems.

Hunger affects entire societies. Here, hungry people in Somalia, in north Africa, fight for precious food.

A wide variety of individuals and organizations have joined the war on hunger. They include scientists, bankers, economists, engineers, doctors, nurses, ministers, and presidents. They face many difficult challenges. How are those on the front line in the war on hunger working to meet these challenges? What are their prospects for future success? This book is about how these individuals and organizations are fighting to solve the problems of serious hunger on Earth.

Chapter 2

Hunger and Poverty

The vast majority of seriously hungry people live in the developing world. According to the World Bank, the developing world is made up of 100 countries located in Central America and Latin America, the Caribbean, the Middle East, Asia, and Africa.[1]

Developing countries are the poorest countries of the world. They're called *developing* because they're striving to develop higher standards of living or quality of life. Of the roughly 6 billion people on Earth at the present time, 5 billion live in the developing world, and 800 million of these people are seriously hungry.[2]

The Gap Between Rich and Poor

Why are so many people in the developing world seriously hungry? It's not because there's too little to eat. The world's farmers grow more than enough crops to meet the minimum daily requirement of 2,500 calories for every single person on Earth. The hungry people in the developing world are hungry because they live in poverty. People who suffer from poverty do not have adequate food, housing, education, health, or work. Many of the world's hungry are farmers who have lost their land and urban dwellers who have no jobs. In the year 2000, about 3 billion people, or half the world's population, lived on an income of less than $2 per day. And more than a billion people, one of every six, lived on less than $1 per day.[3]

These poor people live in a rich world that keeps growing richer. Each year the world's wealth, known as gross national product (GNP), grows. GNP is the total amount of money that the people of one nation earn in a year. During the final decade of the twentieth century, the total GNP of all the nations of the world grew from $31 trillion to $42 trillion.[4]

If this wealth were distributed evenly, everyone would have plenty to eat. But at the present time the richest 1.2 bil-

MAP OPPOSITE:
Developing countries, where hunger is a serious problem, are shown here in light green.

lion people on Earth are 86 times richer than the poorest 1.2 billion. For example, in the year 2000, the average yearly income per person in Japan was $32,350, while in India it was only $440.[5] Year by year this gap between rich and poor keeps growing wider.

Hunger and poverty go hand in hand. To make progress in the war on hunger, the number of people living in poverty must be reduced. Workers in the war on hunger are identifying the problems that lead to poverty and are seeking solutions.

Solving Economic Problems

Some people in developing countries live in poverty because their country's economic system has failed. During the late twentieth century, many poor countries used an economic system called socialism. In a socialist economy, factories, farmland, and businesses are all owned by the central government. It's the government's duty to make sure that everyone gets an equal share of the country's wealth and that no one goes hungry.

In some socialist countries people's standards of living improved during the twentieth century. China is one example. But in many socialist countries, things did not work out as planned. Socialist leaders told people how they must live their lives, how they must do their jobs, and how much they would receive in return for their labor. People were not rewarded for working extra hard or long. A farmer who worked ten hours a day in his field received the same amount of money as a farmer who worked only six hours. Ambition was not rewarded. People did not feel free or in control of their lives. As a result, a great many people did not do their jobs well. They did not produce machinery that worked efficiently. They did not grow enough food.

The biggest socialist economy in the world was the Soviet Union. All through the 1980s this economy was failing, but Soviet leaders insisted on sticking with it. Finally, in 1991, with its economy in ruins, the Soviet Union fell to pieces. The fifteen states that made up the Soviet Union became fifteen separate countries. Today, the standards of living in these fifteen Eastern European republics remain low as people struggle to create new political and economic systems. Many citizens of these republics suffer from serious hunger.

Socialism did not work as planned in the Southeast Asian country of Vietnam either. Starting in the 1970s, Vietnam's socialist leaders ordered farmers to work in cooperatives. In each cooperative, many families had to live together and work their farmland in common, sharing the profits equally.

The problems that resulted in Vietnam were similar to those in the Soviet Union. With the government telling them what to do, people didn't feel in control of their own lives. Because hard work got them no personal reward, they felt no need to work efficiently and well. The result was a low standard of living for most Vietnamese farmers and hunger for many.

Vietnam's leaders saw that people needed to feel more in control of their own lives. So in the mid-1980s, leaders began changing the socialist economy to make it more like a capitalist economy.

In a capitalist economy, such as in the United States, individuals own their own land and work for their own profit. Instead of everyone sharing equally, most people who work harder and more efficiently have the opportunity to become wealthy.

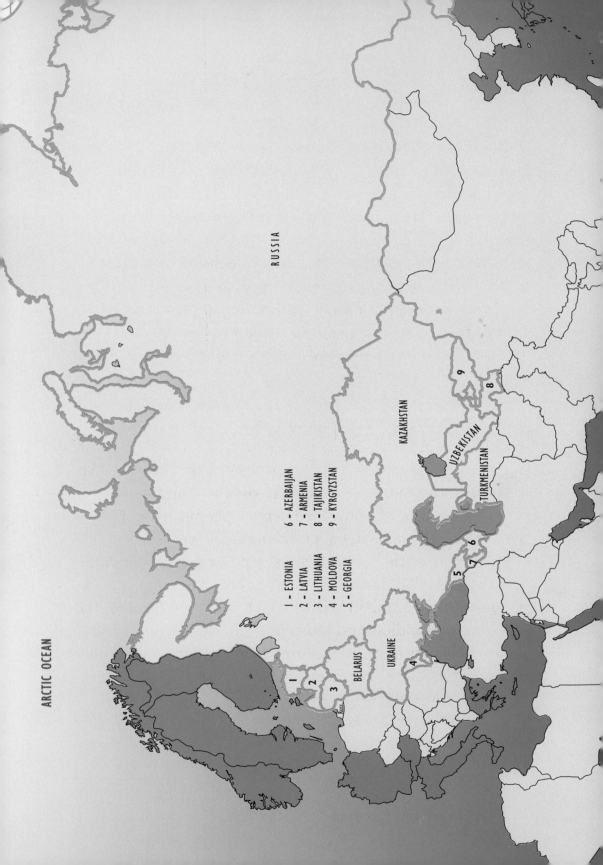

ARCTIC OCEAN

RUSSIA

KAZAKHSTAN

UZBEKISTAN

TURKMENISTAN

BELARUS

UKRAINE

Russia

1 – ESTONIA   6 – AZERBAIJAN
2 – LATVIA   7 – ARMENIA
3 – LITHUANIA   8 – TAJIKISTAN
4 – MOLDOVA   9 – KYRGYZSTAN
5 – GEORGIA

MAP OPPOSITE:

In 1991, when the Soviet Union crumbled, it separated into fifteen different countries, which are now referred to as the Eastern European republics. These countries, labeled here, still suffer from the poverty and serious hunger that was a result of the failed socialist economy.

Vietnam's leaders ordered the farming cooperatives disbanded. Farmers were free to own and work their own farmland and make and keep their own profits. As a result, agricultural productivity rose 50 percent.[6] By reforming their economic system, Vietnam's leaders helped raise people's standard of living, reduce poverty, and fight hunger.

Solving Land Problems

In rich nations, farmers own their land. But in developing countries, most small farmers never own the land they farm. In Haiti, for example, only 3 percent of people living in rural areas own their land. In Egypt, the figure is only 17 percent.[7] Legally, most of the small farmers' land in developing countries belongs to the state, or the national government. The state can seize land and sell it, which it often does, leaving poor farmers landless and hungry.

Governments have seized farmland all over the developing world. In the South American country of Brazil, for example, the number of small farms fell from 3 million in 1985 to less than 1 million in 2000. Much of this land was sold to big landowners. At the present time, 50 percent of Brazil's farmland is owned by less than 2 percent of Brazil's landowners,

CARIBBEAN SEA

BRAZIL

PACIFIC
OCEAN

ATLANTIC
OCEAN

*South America is rampant with farmland
problems. Land reform in Brazil helps
small farmers find unused land to farm.*

and half of that land is not planted with crops. Most of the land lies fallow, unused, while millions of Brazilian farmers are left landless and hungry.[8]

Brazil has a land-reform policy in place. Its constitution states that the government must transfer ownership of some of this fallow land from big landowners to small farmers. Land reform means that small farmers would legally own their land, and the state could no longer seize it from them.

A family of squatters on a Brazilian farm lives in a small tent in hopes that they can take over and farm the unused land.

But Brazil's government has been slow to enforce land reform, so nongovernmental organizations (NGOs) are pushing for land reform. MST (Movimento dos Trabalhadores Rurais Sem Terra, or Landless Workers Movement) is one of these NGOs. To force land reform, MST members stage large-scale occupations.

An occupation works this way: First, MST locates fallow land on a large-scale landowner's farm. Then MST members lead about three hundred farm families to the land. The fam-

MST members are sometimes arrested after occupying unused farmland.

ilies occupy and farm the land until the government grants them legal ownership of the land.

MST's occupations have been successful, but not without violent consequences. Since 1985, some 250,000 families have won legal ownership to land through these occupations, but more than 1,500 MST members and occupying farmers have been assassinated in the process.[9]

Other NGOs in South America, Central America, and Asia are also pushing for land reform. But governments and large-scale landowners are holding onto the land, slowing the pace of land reform in the developing world.

Solving Employment Problems

In developing countries, about 70 percent of the poor live in the countryside. But every day more and more people are migrating to cities in search of work. In the Middle Eastern country of Turkey, three-quarters of the population lived in the countryside fifty years ago. Now, three-quarters of the population lives in cities.[10]

Each day more people come to these cities, but they find no jobs waiting there. So workers in the war on hunger are looking for ways to help rural people remain in the countryside and make a decent living. Peruvian economist Hernando de Soto writes: "It is now time for the West to create new policies that inspire governments to harness the entrepreneurial energy that is already humming among the poor. . . ."[11]

By poor people's "entrepreneurial energy," de Soto means their desire to start their own businesses. Government leaders, NGOs, and banks are helping by giving rural entrepreneurs small, low-interest, microcredit loans.

Beatrice's Good-Luck Goat

One NGO has a unique strategy for fighting the war on hunger in the countryside. Heifer Project International (HPI), based in America, donates food and income-producing animals to farmers in the developing world. When HPI donated a dozen goats to a village in the Central African country of Uganda, one goat went to the family of Beatrice Biira, age nine.

Beatrice badly wanted to go to school. In Uganda, as in most developing countries, public school is not free, and Beatrice's family could not afford to pay the fees for uniforms and books.

Beatrice's mother gave Beatrice the task of taking care of the goat, which the family named Mugisa, the Ugandan word for good fortune. Mugisa did bring good fortune because the goat soon gave birth to

Beatrice says that HPI's goats helped not just her but everyone in her rural Central African village to live their lives free of hunger.

Most microcredit loans go to women. Traditionally, women in the developing world have been denied basic rights granted to men, such as the right to be educated, to own land, and to work. Without a man to support them, many women in the developing world must live in poverty and suffer hunger.

Microcredit loans have changed this. A typical loan is between $25 and $75. In a developing country, this is enough

Beatrice's story is told in a children's book entitled Beatrice's Goat *by Page McBrier. Beatrice attended book signings to promote her story.*

twin kids. There was enough goat's milk to feed the baby goats and to sell to neighbors.

Beatrice's family made enough profit from the milk to pay for a new roof that didn't leak like the old one, new clothes, salt, soap, and manure for the garden. The money also sent Beatrice to school. Beatrice plans to attend college and become a veterinarian one day. She says that HPI's goats helped not just her but everyone in her rural East African village to live their lives free of hunger.

money to start a small business, since the costs of goods and services are much less than in rich countries. NGOs work with government leaders and banks to set up these loans. The NGO known as the Tamil Nadu Women's Development Project, for example, has helped some 70,000 women get microcredit loans from banks in the South Asian country of India. Borrowers use the money to set up small businesses such as poultry farming, handicrafts, or shopkeeping.

Another NGO, Women for Women International, arranges microcredit loans for women in the Eastern European country of Bosnia. One woman, who bought a milk cow with her loan, said, "Everything in my life got better when Women for Women showed up in my village."[12] She used a second loan to buy a second cow and a cheese-making machine. Her income has risen from $57 a month before the loans to $400 a month now.

Chapter 3

Hunger and the Environment

The majority of hungry people in the developing world are farmers. But they're different from farmers in rich nations. They don't own large tracts of rich land where they grow crops to sell at a profit. And they don't use tractors and other farm machinery.

Instead, most farmers in the developing world work small plots of land by hand. They use oxen or mules to pull their plows. They plant, water, weed, and harvest by hand. And instead of selling their crops for a profit, most of these farmers can only hope to produce enough to feed themselves. They're called subsistence farmers. They grow food to subsist, or survive.

Some subsistence farmers also raise livestock. They might raise cows for milk, sheep for wool, chickens for eggs, or pigs

A subsistence farmer in Vietnam must work hard to feed his family.

for meat. Whether they grow crops or raise livestock or do both, subsistence farmers struggle to produce enough food to live on.

In good times, they succeed. But these farmers are poorly prepared for bad weather and natural disasters. They don't have savings or insurance to help them through bad times. In bad times, they often go hungry.

Subsistence farming has always been a tough way to make a living, and it's getting tougher each year. Good farmland in developing countries is harder to find. One reason for this is the growing number of people in the world.

Combating Desertification

Presently there are about 6.2 billion people on Earth. By 2015, that number is estimated to increase by about 1 billion, and nearly all that increase is predicted to take place in the developing world.[1]

That means that developing-world farmers will have to grow more and more food to feed more and more people. But there is only so much farmland on Earth. Just 10 percent of the Earth's land surface is arable—that is, suitable for growing crops. The rest of the land is covered by cities or mountains, or is too cold or too dry to farm. The amount of arable land shrinks each year. It's covered up by cities that keep growing.

Farmers need good, fertile land and a steady supply of water to successfully grow crops. It makes sense, then, that farmers will take good care of the land and water. But sometimes, in trying to make use of land and water, farmers end up damaging the vital resources they must have to survive.

As mentioned in chapter 1, many subsistence farmers lose their land to the state. Some of them give up farming and move to cities. But others resort to farming on drylands that no one else wants because they are too dry to grow crops.

Farmers may succeed in scratching out a living for a while on drylands. But very few crops can be grown successfully. Farmers who try to grow crops unsuited to this dry soil soon destroy the drylands. Precious topsoil is lost through erosion, and the land becomes a desert. This process is called desertification. The end results are damage to the environment and more poverty and hunger.

Sheep and cattle have overgrazed this pasture so that it's on the verge of becoming desert land. Soon there will be no food left for this farmer's livestock.

The UN Office to Combat Desertification and Drought works with governments to stop the destruction of drylands. This organization helps governments identify where drylands are located and directs farmers to land that is more suitable for raising crops.

The Global Information and Early Warning System (GIEWS) is an important tool for combating desertification. It was established by the UN in 1975. GIEWS collects and analyzes information from 115 governments and 61 NGOs around the world. Its information includes soil, water, and weather conditions. Reports go out to members, warning them of land areas in danger of becoming desertified.

NGOs also combat desertification by working directly with farmers. For example, the International Institute of Tropical Agriculture in Nigeria, West Africa, has shown farmers how to grow cassava, a root vegetable that can be grown in drylands without destroying topsoil. Growing cassava on drylands has helped reduce the number of hungry people in developing countries in Africa, Asia, and South America.

Irrigating With Freshwater

Farmers can't depend on rain to water their crops because weather is too unpredictable. They can't be sure their crops will get enough rainfall to grow. So they irrigate their crops. An estimated one-third of the world's food supply comes from irrigated land.[2] Most irrigation is done by pumping freshwater from underground or by diverting it from rivers or streams and then running it along ditches between rows of crops. This system is known as flood irrigation.

Farmers need a great deal of freshwater to irrigate their land. For example, it takes 1,000 tons of freshwater to produce a ton of wheat.[3] Farmers get their irrigation water from two sources: the water table and fossil water.

The water table is water in the earth that can be replaced by rainwater and melted snow. Fossil water is water contained in underground reservoirs, which are natural, open spaces enclosed by rock. No rivers or streams run into these reservoirs. Once fossil water is pumped up and out of reservoirs, it's gone forever.

As the Earth's population grows, freshwater becomes harder to find. Reservoirs of fossil water become empty as people pump water out. Water tables fall as people use water faster than nature can replace it. Then farmers no longer have enough freshwater to meet their irrigation needs. They must compete with each other for every drop.

Besides competing with each other for irrigation water, farmers must compete with cities. With more people moving to developing-world cities every day, more freshwater must go to cities and less to farmers in the countryside.

With less freshwater available, farmers must find ways to grow their crops with less water. Drip irrigation uses less water than flood systems. In drip irrigation, water is released gradually through tubes and hoses at root level. Drip irrigation is also more productive. Farmland often yields more crops from drip irrigation than from flooding.

NGOs are designing, producing, and selling low-cost drip irrigation systems to small-scale farmers in the developing world. An NGO known as International Development Enterprises (IDE) helps develop low-cost irrigation systems and helps small-scale farmers get microcredit loans to buy them.

This deep well was dug to irrigate the community's vegetable fields in Mali, in northwest Africa.

A small drip-irrigation kit uses just two buckets of water a day to grow a home garden.

The treadle pump is another low-cost irrigation tool that's catching on fast. More than a million treadle pumps have been sold in Asia alone. They are operated by foot pedals. By pedaling them, farmers pull water up out of the ground from a narrow well made from a metal tube.

These irrigation systems are not expensive. Many subsistence farmers have been able to buy them with microcredit loans. Dangi Marandi, a farmer from India, said, "I have a small piece of land on which I cultivate vegetables. I used to work on my field all day long, and carry water from the nearest pond with pitchers for irrigation." Then she got a treadle pump. The pump "is a machine that provided me self-sufficiency and confidence as well as a bright future for my family."[4]

In India, Dangi Marandi uses an inexpensive treadle pump, which allows her to be independent and self-sufficient after her husband deserted her and her daughter. The extra income she generates allows her to provide better living conditions for her daughter and sufficient health care for both of them.

Factory Fishing Heads South

Globally, about one billion people depend on fish and other marine life as their primary source of animal protein, and the number grows each day. As the world's population grows, the demand for food from the sea also grows.

Massive ships known as fishing factory trawlers pull tons of marine life from the ocean's depths. Until 1989, these trawlers worked primarily in the oceans of the Northern Hemisphere, off the shores of rich nations.

Then, as experts put it, the fishing industry hit the wall. The oceans of the north could no longer keep up with the world's demand for marine life. So some of these trawlers headed south to waters off the coasts of developing countries in South America, Asia, and Africa. By the year 2000, nearly 50 percent of the fish caught worldwide came from oceans bordering developing countries.[5] This was not good news for local fishers in developing countries.

Big Fishers Swallow Little Fishers

Subsistence fishers are like subsistence farmers. They work to feed themselves and their families. During good times, subsistence fishers succeed. During bad times, they go hungry.

When factory trawlers began working the coasts of developing countries in the 1990s, the lives of many subsistence fishers changed for the worse. The trawlers were fishing close to shore where subsistence fishers worked. The supply of marine life got so low that subsistence fishers could no longer make a living. Their catch had been taken by the trawlers.

A fishing trawler operation (above) is clearly capable of catching a lot more fish than individual subsistence fishers (below). Many trawlers are depleting the amount of fish available to local fishers, who need the food to survive.

To make matters worse, most of the marine life that trawlers take is exported to rich nations. As a result, people in many developing countries can no longer buy fish to eat. An important source of nutritious, low-cost food is gone for those who need it most.

An NGO Protests

Some NGOs devote themselves to lobbying. They work to persuade, or lobby, government leaders to help their cause. The NGO known as the Creed Alliance, based in Pakistan, is dedicated to saving the environment. As part of its work, this organization helps subsistence fishers. Aly Ercelawn, a Creed leader, protested to the government of Pakistan that fishing trawlers from China and Korea were invading the waters of Pakistan's local fishers. Ercelawn asked government leaders to ban trawlers from the waters of local fishers.

Although Creed did not persuade Pakistan's leaders to help subsistence fishers, this NGO continued to lobby for its cause.

Aquaculture Problems

The end of the twentieth century saw a rapid rise in fish farming, which is called *aquaculture*. Today, more than one-fourth of the fish and other marine life that people consume is produced by aquaculture.

Some fish farms are ponds constructed along coastlines that were once covered by mangroves. Mangroves are tropical trees whose thick roots reach down into the water. Mangrove forests have been called rain forests by the sea because they provide homes for marine life, birds, monkeys, lizards, and sea turtles.

Many of the world's mangrove forests have been destroyed to make way for fish farms. The result is the loss of homes for marine, bird, and animal life. Fish farms also destroy valuable farmland. Many aquaculture ponds need a mix of freshwater and salt water. The salt from the fish ponds gets into the freshwater supply and pollutes nearby farmland, ruining it for the growing of crops.

National governments and NGOs are taking steps to deal with these problems. In India, for example, there are NGOs composed of people dedicated to repairing environmental damage. These environmental activists have helped to influence India's government to order the closing of 100,000 acres (40,470 hectares) of shrimp farms.

Dryland farming, factory fishing, and aquaculture are all meant to help feed people. But if valuable land and water sources are destroyed in the process, there will be more hunger in the long run, not less.

Chapter 4

Hunger and Politics

Weather-related problems, such as droughts and floods, are not the chief causes of hunger. In a world that could have plenty of food for everyone, the chief causes of hunger lie with people, not nature. George McGovern, U.S. ambassador to the UN's Food and Agriculture Organization, wrote that "hunger is a political condition."[1] He meant that political and business leaders sometimes make decisions and pass laws that contribute to the problem of hunger in the world.

The Problem of Factory Farms

Grains are the most nutritious form of low-cost food on Earth. That's why subsistence farmers grow mostly grains, such as wheat, rice, and corn. Poor people in the developing world depend on these nutritious, low-cost grains for survival.

As mentioned in chapter 1, many subsistence farmers are losing their farmland to the state. The state then sells or leases this farmland to large corporations in rich nations, which turn vast tracts of land into factory farms. Factory farms are worked by local people using modern machinery. The crops grown on factory farms are sold in rich nations. The land that once grew grain for local people now grows crops for faraway people in rich nations.

The result is a shortage of grain for poor countries, which means that poor countries must import grain from other countries to meet their people's needs. But grain grown in other countries is more expensive than grain grown locally. Poor people in developing countries typically spend about 70 percent of their income on food.[2] So even a small increase in food prices makes a big difference to them, and those who can't afford to pay the higher price for imported grain go hungry.

The Problem of Trade Limits

Nations export and import goods, such as crops and clothing, all the time. To *export* means *to send out*. A nation exports its goods by shipping them out to a foreign nation where those goods are sold. To *import* means *to take in*. A nation imports goods by taking in goods from a foreign nation for its people to buy. When nations export and import goods, they are trading with each other.

Trade is vital for poor nations. They can produce and sell goods such as clothing and furniture at lower prices than rich nations. This is because workers in poor countries are paid less for their labor than workers in rich nations. If not for trade with rich nations, many workers in poor countries would not have jobs and would go hungry.

But workers in rich nations also produce goods such as clothing and furniture. These workers don't want lower-priced exports from poor countries to hurt their businesses. So rich nations set trade limits on foreign goods through tariffs and quotas.

Tariffs are taxes on imports, and quotas are limits on how much a nation will agree to take in. By setting trade limits, rich nations make it difficult for poor nations to make a profit exporting their goods. Rich nations have pledged to help poor nations by engaging in free trade—that is, by eliminating tariffs and quotas on the goods of poor nations. But they have not always followed through on this pledge because workers in rich nations fear losing their jobs. This could happen in the United States if Americans buy fewer products made at home.

The Need for Free Trade

What would free trade mean to a developing country? Pakistan is a good example. After the terrorist attacks of September 11, 2001, U.S. orders for clothing and other textiles from Pakistan fell sharply as part of a general slowdown in

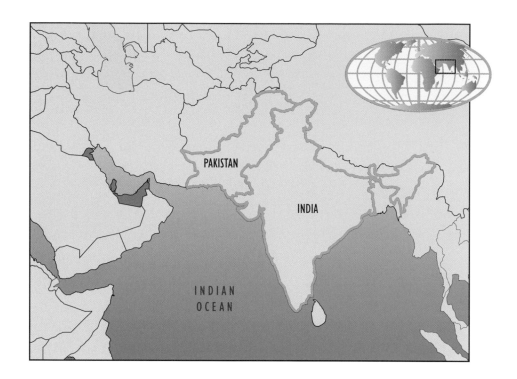

the U.S. economy. As a result, an estimated 18,000 workers in Pakistan's textile industry lost their jobs, and no jobs often means that people go hungry.

Before September 11, the U.S. government had put a 17.5 percent tariff on Pakistani textile imports. Members of the Textile and Apparel Group, a Pakistani NGO, lobbied the U.S. government to suspend this tariff. If the tariff were suspended, Pakistan could price their textiles lower and sell more of them in the United States. Then Pakistan could rehire the workers who had lost their jobs. A spokesman for the group said, "Pakistan desperately needs tariff relief for our industry to survive."[3] Without it, more workers would lose their jobs and their ability to feed their families.

But the U.S. textile industry protested. It used its influence to keep the U.S. government from suspending the tariff.

Like other rich nations, America has pledged to engage in free trade. But home industries put pressure on their national governments to resist. As a result, the United States and other rich nations still have not made good on their pledge of free trade.

Less Aid and More Debt

Since the early 1970s, rich nations have been giving poor countries billions of dollars of aid to fight hunger. But during the 1990s and into the twenty-first century, rich nations cut back on this aid. Poor nations have asked rich nations to contribute 0.7 percent of their gross national product as aid. As of 2001, rich nations contributed only 0.24 percent of their GNP as aid. The United States was on the low end, contributing only 0.1 percent of its GNP, an average of $29 per person.[4] Sweden was on the high end, contributing a full 1 percent of its GNP, an average of $260 per person.[5]

Poor nations have also received help in the form of loans from national governments and from international banks, such as the World Bank. The loans were intended to help fight the war on hunger by giving poor countries the resources to raise their people's standard of living.

Some poor countries have used the money as intended, such as Mexico, the Philippines, and much of Latin America. But some have used it to equip armies to fight wars instead of fight hunger. Other countries have had their food-aid money stolen by corrupt leaders. In the 1980s, President Mobutu Sese Seko of the central African country of Zaire (now the Democratic Republic of the Congo) managed to put an esti-

ARCTIC OCEAN

PACIFIC
OCEAN

AUSTRALIA

INDIAN OCEAN

SWEDEN

FINLAND

GREECE

1 - DENMARK
2 - NETHERLANDS
3 - BELGIUM
4 - LUXEMBOURG
5 - GERMANY
6 - AUSTRIA

5

1

2

3

4

6

ITALY

FRANCE

SPAIN

NORTHERN
IRELAND

IRELAND

GREAT
BRITAIN

PORTUGAL

CANADA

UNITED STATES

ATLANTIC OCEAN

PACIFIC OCEAN

MAP OPPOSITE:

The richer countries, labeled here, are also known as industrialized nations. They lend money to developing countries to fight hunger and other social problems. This creates a large amount of debt that the poorer countries have to pay back.

mated $5 billion of aid and loan money into his own personal bank accounts.[6] He used some of it to build castles and palaces for himself in eight different countries. None of it went to fight hunger in his desperately poor country.

NGOs Lobby for Debt Relief

Some poor countries are hopelessly in debt. Some NGOs are working to persuade national governments and international banks to forgive loans to these desperately poor countries. In April 2000, for example, thousands of members of an international NGO called Jubilee 2000 gathered on the Mall in Washington, D.C. They locked arms in a protest reported in news media around the world. Their human chain, they explained, symbolized the "chains of debt" that financially enslave poor nations to rich ones.

These NGOs are lobbying rich nations to wipe away the debts of the heavily indebted poor countries. These countries have no hope of ever paying back the loans, NGOs say. The amount that poor countries owe increases each year because of interest, which is the extra cost paid to lenders for the temporary use of their money. For example, the countries of Zambia and Mozambique, in southern Africa, spend more on

After the Jubilee 2000 protest in Washington, D.C., citizens in many other countries held similar protests. Here, protesters gather in London, England, to demand that Western countries cancel developing-world debt.

paying back the interest on these loans than they spend on education, clean water, health services, and nutrition combined. In the meantime, these countries can't make any progress in fighting serious hunger.

These NGOs have had some success. International banks and national governments have been persuaded to forgive some of the debts of the most highly indebted poor nations. Rich nations have shown that they really do want to help end hunger. But they also want to become richer themselves. That's why they run factory farms in poor nations and don't grant free trade. Unfortunately, when rich nations do these things, they contribute to world hunger instead of fighting it.

Chapter 5

Hunger and the Use of Force

Many of the poorest countries with the most hungry people are not run by democratically elected leaders. They are run by dictators — people who have taken power, often by force.

Elected officials must respond to the needs of the people or risk being voted out of office. But dictators don't face this risk. Instead of working to share the country's wealth, they grab it for themselves, to help keep themselves in power.

Dictators control the nations' newspapers and radio and TV stations. They severely limit free speech. They make sure that the nations' media tell people only what they, the dictators, want the people to hear. Dictators seldom permit opposition and often punish anyone who dares oppose them. One of the weapons that dictators use to punish their opponents is hunger.

A Leader Uses Hunger as a Weapon

Saddam Hussein of Iraq is a dictator who has used hunger as a weapon against his opponents, the Madan, also known as the marsh Arabs. Since ancient times the Madan have lived in the marshes of southern Iraq, building islands and houses of reeds and making their living by hunting and fishing.

The Madan opposed Hussein but kept quiet about their feelings until 1991 when the United States fought Iraq in the Persian Gulf War. When Iraq invaded neighboring Kuwait, America sent troops to get Iraq out of Kuwait. The Madan voiced their support for the United States and their opposition to Saddam Hussein. The United States won the war and drove Hussein's Iraqi troops out of Kuwait, but Hussein remained as Iraq's dictator.

To punish the Madan for opposing him, Hussein ordered canals built and river waters diverted to dry up the Madan's marshes. From 1991 to 2001, 90 percent of the Madan's marshes dried up, killing the fish, which were the Madan's primary source of food and income.[1] Many hungry Madan were forced to flee to neighboring countries. Hussein sent troops to destroy the Madan's villages and drive the rest of them out of Iraq.

Holding Leaders Responsible

A key weapon in the war on world hunger is a democratic government made up of leaders elected by the people. George McGovern wrote: "World hunger can't be ended unless the developing countries achieve more responsible governments.

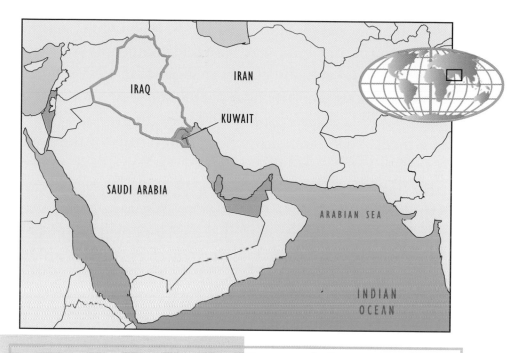

By eliminating the Madan people's source of food, Saddam Hussein forced them out of southern Iraq into neighboring countries.

This calls for a greater measure of democracy with political rights, and a responsiveness to basic human needs."[2]

One developing country that responds to the needs of its people in terms of hunger is India. India is a democracy. Its leaders are elected by the people. It is also a desperately poor country whose people experience serious hunger in great numbers.

But hunger in India was much worse in the past. India used to experience famines, which are periods of time when great numbers of people die of starvation. Famine in India was confined to regions of the country where no food was available.

In these regions, people starved to death. Meanwhile, in other regions, a surplus of food was available and people were well fed. In fact, India actually exported some of its rice, selling it to other countries while its own people starved.

Why couldn't India's leaders find ways to prevent famine? Indian media reporters and political opponents of the country's leaders kept asking this question. The answer seemed to be that India's leaders were not willing to respond to the needs of the people.

But these outspoken reporters and political opponents kept putting pressure on India's leaders to deal with the threat of famine. Soon, these leaders realized that if they did not deal with the problem, they would be voted out of office. So they took action. India still experiences a great deal of serious hunger. But the government now has emergency plans in place. At the first sign of a possible famine, the government transports surplus food supplies to the people who need them.

Conflicts Cause Hunger

Most leaders of poor countries come to power by force, so they are accustomed to using force to get what they want. The use of force often leads to armed conflict: civil wars and wars with neighboring nations. With so many poor countries headed by dictators, armed conflicts are common in the developing world.

Some of these armed conflicts last for years on end. In the Democratic Republic of the Congo, years of civil war have taken nearly 3 million lives. But according to a survey conducted by the International Rescue Committee (IRC), the vast majority of casualties in this war were not soldiers. They were innocent civilians, who died from disease and starvation caused by the conflict raging around them.[3]

Relief Agencies Try to Help

NGOs deliver emergency food supplies to civilians in countries engaged in armed conflict. Most emergency food comes from international relief agencies such as CARE, based in America; Oxfam, based in Great Britain; the International Red Cross; and the United Nations World Food Program (WFP). Relief agencies face a huge challenge. At any single time, tens of millions of people in dozens of countries face food emergencies.

The funds to purchase and deliver emergency food are donated by individuals and governments of rich nations. The United States is the largest donor.

But rich nations have been cutting back on their donations to relief agencies. During the 1990s, donations dropped more than 20 percent. Rich nations complain that corrupt leaders in developing countries are misusing food aid.

Some leaders intercept food meant to be given to seriously hungry people, and then sell it at a profit to become wealthy. Other corrupt leaders block emergency food supplies from reaching the people who need them. Leaders of the North African country of Sudan have done this. Sudan, an extremely poor country, has been ravaged by an ongoing civil war with rebel forces battling ruling government forces. Sudan's leaders block emergency food supplies from reaching

The WFP provides emerency food aid
to the people of Afghanistan.

any communities suspected of supporting rebel forces. As a result, millions of Sudan's people live under the constant threat of starvation.

No Simple Solutions

There are no simple solutions for winning the battle against world hunger in poor countries. No matter how much food is available and no matter how hard people try to distribute it to those who most need it, political problems stand in the way.

Before serious hunger can be brought under control in poor countries, government leaders must be held accountable for their actions. They must be voted into office through free and open elections. Then, if they do not respond to the needs of the people, they can be voted out of office. But dictators who seize power, such as Saddam Hussein of Iraq and Mobutu Sese Seko of Zaire, can't be voted out of office. Democratic governments with elected public officials are far more likely to be responsive to the needs of the people they lead.

Hunger has not been eliminated in democratic nations either. The war on hunger is fought in rich nations, too, including the United States.

Chapter 6

Hunger in the United States

There have always been hungry people in the United States, but the American public has not always been aware of this fact. It wouldn't be much of an exaggeration to say that before the 1960s, the only people who knew there were hungry people in the United States were the hungry Americans themselves.

Americans in the 1960s knew that there were hundreds of millions of hungry people in the developing world. But most Americans saw themselves as living in a land of plenty where no one ever went hungry. After all, the United States had one of the highest standards of living in the world.

It still does. The United States was and is a land of plenty—including plenty of waste. Every year Americans throw away more than a quarter of their food supplies.[1] Grocery stores throw away fruits and vegetables and baked

There are millions of people in the United States who don't have enough income to provide themselves with a decent meal.

goods that don't sell. Restaurants throw away tons of uneaten food. The same thing happens in school and hospital cafeterias. How could there possibly be hungry people in a nation that has more food than it knows what to do with?

Americans "Discover" Hunger

A few government leaders in the 1960s were aware of the hunger problem at home, and they launched an investigation. Teams of doctors and nutrition experts were sent on field trips to poor sections of the nation looking for hungry Americans. They found millions of them. In a 1967 report to the

U.S. Congress they wrote: "We have found concrete evidence of chronic hunger and malnutrition in every part of the U.S. where we have held hearings or conducted field trips."[2]

A television program also played a role in alerting Americans to hunger in their own land. On May 21, 1968, CBS TV broadcast the documentary *Hunger in America.* Camera crews went out all over the United States to document the lives of hungry Americans. This real-life program revealed that 25 million Americans were suffering from hunger and malnutrition.

To many Americans, the news was shocking. One scene in particular caught people's attention. It was an interview with a boy in a lunchroom who was watching his classmates eat their school lunches. The boy himself had nothing to eat. In the 1960s the federal government provided low-cost school lunches. But many Americans, like the boy, couldn't afford them. A reporter asked the boy how he felt, watching his classmates eat when he had nothing. The boy answered, "I feel ashamed." After the broadcast, one government official said, "It was I, a U.S. senator living in comfort, who should feel ashamed that there were hungry people—young and old—in my own beloved country."[3]

Who Is Hungry in the United States?

The percentage of Americans who suffer from hunger is much lower than in the developing world. And few Americans die of hunger-related illnesses today. But at the present time, some 31 million Americans do not have access to enough food on a daily basis to lead active, healthy lives.[4] These Americans are not in danger of starvation, but they can't always be sure where their next meal is coming from.

Profiles of Hungry Americans

Who are the hungry Americans? Here are some examples.

- An elderly couple who have worked hard their whole lives but whose life savings has been wiped out by sudden, unexpected medical bills.
- A woman and her daughter, both struggling with mental illness, who can't hold down jobs and be productive members of society.
- A family of six struggling to feed themselves because the parents have been laid off from their jobs.
- A single mother who must choose whether to spend her remaining money to buy food or pay the rent because she works a minimum-wage job and pays for day care for her two young children.

Now, as in the 1960s, Americans are hungry for a variety of reasons. As in the developing world, most of these reasons are tied to poverty. Currently, the U.S. government defines poverty as a family of four earning less than $16,895 a year. Using this figure, about 13 percent of the U.S. population lives in poverty.[5]

A great many Americans who suffer from hunger work in full-time, unskilled jobs that pay minimum wage. The minimum wage is the lowest hourly rate that an employer is required by the government to pay an employee. Minimum-wage workers include house cleaners, yard workers, and store clerks. Some work two jobs. But many minimum-wage workers still can't make enough money to pay rent and medical bills, buy clothes for their children, afford a car to get to and from work, and still have enough left over to pay for food.

As in the developing world, many American families are hungry due to poverty, homelessness, and unemployment.

Fighting Hunger in Schools

Children are especially vulnerable to the effects of hunger. Each year in America, 9 million children receive some kind of emergency food help. Hunger expert J. Larry Brown of Tufts University says that hunger robs children of their God-given potential. "We deliver them to the schoolhouse door with one arm tied behind their backs and expect teachers to perform an often-impossible task. This, in turn, results in the waste of billions of dollars we invest in the education of our children because hunger prevents so many of them from getting the full value of their educational experience."[6]

After hunger in the United States was "discovered" in the 1960s, the school-lunch program was improved, and in some schools a breakfast program was added. During the 1999–2000 school year, more than 15 million children received free or reduced-price meals through the National School Lunch Program. Some of these children depend on these meals for a healthy existence. Studies show that government meals provide between one-third and one half of the nutrients that low-income children consume every weekday during the school year.

Fighting Hunger at Home

To help hungry families, the government set up the Food Stamp Program in the 1960s. Families whose income falls below the official poverty level are eligible to receive a certain amount of money each month in the form of food stamps. The stamps are meant to supply families with the additional nourishment they need to live healthy lives. The stamps work like money. Recipients present them to the cashier at the grocery-store checkout.

But the Food Stamp Program has a history of problems. Between 1994 and 1999, the number of people receiving food stamps dropped by 10 million. Presently, only about half the people eligible for food stamps are actually enrolled.

One reason for the low enrollment is the process that people must go through to apply for food stamps. Applications for food stamps in most states are long and complex. They ask the applicant to supply a number of legal documents that may be difficult to obtain. And the process is lengthy and costly, requiring many applicants to travel long distances and take time off from work, which means lost wages that they can't afford to give up.

Pride is another reason for low enrollment. In surveys, many Americans admit that they are either too embarrassed or too proud to be seen using food stamps in grocery stores.

Government officials are tackling the pride problem by replacing the paper stamps with electronic transfer benefit cards, which look and work like credit cards. Instead of receiving stamps, people are credited with their benefits in a bank account. They present their benefit cards instead of stamps, at grocery stores, to purchase food. Officials hope that when eligible people who are not receiving benefits see the cards, they will change their minds and enroll in the program.

U.S. NGOs Fight the War on Hunger

Nongovernmental organizations fight the war on hunger in the United States, just as they fight it in the developing world. Here are some examples.

Food providers

Some NGOs work to provide canned goods and hot meals to hungry Americans. Food pantries provide canned goods. Soup kitchens provide hot meals. No one knows the number of food providers at work in the United States, but it is estimated in the hundreds of thousands.

These NGOs are run almost entirely by volunteers, who give their time and energy freely to cook and distribute food to the hungry. The largest of America's NGO food providers is

This soup kitchen is at the Holy Apostles Church in New York City. Volunteers served an overwhelming number of hungry and homeless because unemployment rose sharply in the wake of the terrorist attacks on the World Trade Center.

Second Harvest. Each year this organization distributes more than a billion pounds of donated food and grocery products to local charities and food programs across the United States.

Gleaners

Some NGOs, known as gleaners, rescue wasted food and distribute it to the hungry. Originally, the term *gleaner* meant people who gather grain left behind on farm fields during harvesttime. Modern gleaners in cities collect food that otherwise would go to waste.

As mentioned earlier, Americans throw away more than a quarter of their food stock each year. No government program has been set up to collect the vast amount of canned and packaged foods, baked goods, and fresh fruits and vegetables discarded every day by bakeries, hospitals, restaurants, and grocery stores. So gleaners have moved in to do the job. New York's City Harvest, as one example, arranges with these institutions to pick up their excess food each day. City Harvest does not accept food that has already been served. Trucks collect the food and deliver it to soup kitchens and food pantries in and around New York City. This NGO also accepts private donations of money and nonperishable food items.

Lobbying Groups

Some NGOs spend their time and energies lobbying, appealing to government officials to favor more aid to hungry people. These lobbying groups also ask the public to help them persuade government officials to provide hungry people with jobs.

One of these lobbying groups is Bread for the World. This organization believes that providing hungry people with food is only half the battle. Its 45,000 members contact their senators and representatives about laws concerning hungry people, both in the United States and worldwide. They believe that "food assistance is less important to overcoming hunger than job opportunities. Empowering people, providing them with opportunities or helping them cultivate an awareness of what they can do to improve their lives, is one of the most important ways of overcoming hunger and poverty."[7]

Chapter 7

Moving Toward a Better World

Beginning in the 1960s, research scientists began finding new ways to make farming more productive. Through the end of the twentieth century, they continued to develop new varieties of plants along with new fertilizers and pesticides that helped farmers improve their crop yield, or grow more food per acre.

Together, these scientific breakthroughs became known as the Green Revolution. This revolution continues. Today's research scientists have found a startling new way to improve crop yields. They can actually modify a plant's genes.

Genes are tiny parts of cells that control the way living things grow and behave. All the genes of a living thing taken together are its genome. By modifying a plant's genome, scientists can modify that plant's behavior. Research scientists have used gene modification to produce a variety of plants, known as genetically modified organisms (GMOs), that are more resistant to insects and drought.

For example, research scientists in India have created a new variety of genetically modified chickpea. This vegetable has long supplied nutritious food to millions of hungry people in India. But until recently a tiny insect kept the chickpea yield down. This insect, the pod borer, bores its way into the chickpea and eats it from the inside out. A serious attack by these insects could ruin a farmer's entire crop. Because of the pod borer, some farmers and their families were going hungry.

Then Indian research scientists discovered a way to neutralize the pod borer. They inserted genes from other plants,

Chickpeas provide millions of hungry people in developing countries with a low-cost source of nutrition. Here, a man sells chickpeas at a roadside stand in Turkey.

the peanut and the windbean, into the chickpea. This caused the chickpea to change its behavior and begin manufacturing a new chemical. This chemical kept the pod borer from being able to digest the chickpea. Almost overnight, pod borers stopped eating chickpeas, and the average yield of chickpeas per acre doubled.

GMOs such as the new Indian chickpea promise more crops per acre, but not everyone is in favor of growing them. Anti-GMO groups in Europe and the United States say that GMOs could be dangerous. It's true that no GMOs have been known to cause harm to human health. But since they're a new species, the effects of GMOs on other living things can't be predicted with absolute certainty.

Producing more crops per acre continues to be an important strategy in the war on hunger. But we know that increasing crop yields alone will not win this war. There is already enough food in the world to feed everyone, yet nearly a billion people still suffer from serious hunger. Other key problems must be solved.

Keys to Fighting the War on Hunger

As mentioned earlier in this book, the number of seriously hungry people in the world is dropping by about 6 million per year. But at that rate it would take more than a century to eliminate serious hunger in the world.

People fighting the war on hunger are not willing to wait that long. Making progress in the war on hunger within the next two decades means coming to grips with two other difficult problems examined earlier: poverty and politics.

Poverty

World population is expected to rise to 8 billion by 2030 and 10 billion by 2050.[1] Experts say that farmers should be able to keep growing enough food to feed everyone. But this food won't help the hungry people who can't gain access to it because they are unable to make a decent living. Today, half the world's population survives on less than $2 a day per person. If this situation doesn't improve, world hunger will continue to be a problem no matter how much food the world produces.

International organizations, national governments, and NGOs are working to reduce poverty so that everyone can make a decent living. And they are making some progress through such strategies as land reform, microcredit, low-cost irrigation technologies, and repairing environmental damage.

Politics

As mentioned earlier in this book, rich nations remain reluctant to grant poor nations free trade and forgive their debts. Poor nations remain burdened with leaders who are not responsive to the needs of their people and who engage in disastrous armed conflicts that leave millions homeless and hungry.

Good News, Bad News

The good news, then, is that the world continues to produce an abundance of food. The bad news is that hundreds of millions of people continue to be denied access to this abundance. Meanwhile, the war on hunger continues, with a wide variety of individuals and organizations looking for new and better ways to produce more food and distribute it to the people who need it most.

How You Can Help

Every day, young people help fight the war on hunger. Here are strategies they're using, strategies that you can use, too.

Writing Letters

You can write letters to alert people to the knowledge you have gained about the causes of serious hunger and how they can be solved. You can write to newspaper editors, who sometimes publish letters from readers. You can also write to elected officials in your town and state, such as your mayor or town council and your state and national representatives and senators. Part of an elected official's job is to read and reply to letters about issues such as world hunger.

Students can collect donations at their schools to send to food providers.

Volunteering

You can volunteer your time to help out at a local food provider. Check to see whether there is a soup kitchen or a food pantry near you, and talk to someone in charge about the kind of help they need.

Raising Funds and Food

You can help raise money. Middle-school and high-school classes all over the United States have gotten together to hold fund-raising events, such as bake sales and flea markets, to raise money for local food providers. You can also donate the money you raise to buy emergency food supplies for victims of natural disasters, such as earthquakes and droughts. These Web sites offer information on volunteering time and donating money to fight hunger:

www.mercycorps.org/
www.kids.maine.org/

For Further Information

A great deal of information on world hunger is available on the World Wide Web. You can use a search engine, such as Google, Alta Vista, or Yahoo, to call up lists of Web sites. Try some key words like these:

aquaculture

developing countries

drylands farming

factory farms

famine

food pantries

genetically modified organisms

hunger

malnutrition

subsistence farming

The following Web sites are especially good for picking up a broad range of information on different aspects of world hunger.

Food and Agriculture Organization of the United Nations
www.fao.org/
This UN organization is dedicated to fighting hunger worldwide. Its Web site includes a feature called "Global Watch," which gives late-breaking information on food crises around the world.

Food Research and Action Center (FRAC)
www.frac.org/
This nonprofit organization is dedicated to reducing hunger in the United States. The Web site brings together information about hunger in the United States from thousands of individuals and organizations across the country.

Global Movement for Children
www.gmfc.org/en/index_html
This worldwide organization of NGOs is dedicated to promoting the rights of the child. The site has sections on protecting children from war, disease, and hunger.

Oxfam America
www.oxfamamerica.org/education/
Oxfam (Oxford Committee for Famine Relief) is an international charity dedicated to helping people move out of poverty. The Oxfam Web site is aimed at young people. It includes educational games, classroom activities, videos, and fact sheets about fighting the war on hunger in the United States and around the world.

United Nations Conference on Trade and Development
www.unctad.org/en/subsites/ldcs/country/country.htm
This section of the UN site gives statistical profiles of developing countries.

United Nations Cyberschoolbus
www.un.org/pubs/cyberschoolbus/
This UN Web site gives young people a look at how the United Nations works. The site includes statistics on all the member nations.

End Notes

Chapter 1

1. Food and Agriculture Organization of the United Nations. The State of Food Insecurity in the World 2000. www.fao.org/DOCREP/X8200E/x8200e03.htm#TopofPage, 2000, p. 13.

2. Food and Agriculture Organization of the United Nations. At the World Agricultural Forum, in St. Louis, Missouri. www.fao.org/WAICENT/OIS/PRESS_NE/PRESSENG/2001/pren0132.htm, May 20, 2001.

3. Food and Agriculture Organization of the United Nations. The State of Food Insecurity in the World 2000, p. 13.

4. Food and Agriculture Organization of the United Nations. The State of Food Insecurity in the World 2000, p. iv.

5. Julia Spry-Leverton. Hunger strikes at the heart of family life. UNICEF. www.unicef.org/somalia/inforsect/rabdstory.html, April 15, 2000.

6. UNICEF. State of the World's Children 1998. www.unicef.org/sowc98/silent.htm.

7. The World Food Conference in Rome. Universal Declaration on the Eradication of Hunger and Malnutrition. www.unhchr.ch/html/menu3/b/69.htm, 1974.

8. Food and Agricultural Organization of the United Nations. Speaking Before Representatives from FAO's 183 Member States, Jacques Diouf Denounces the Tragedy of Hunger in A World of Abundance. www.fao.org/WAICENT/OIS/PRESS_NE/2001/pren0180.htm, November 3, 2001.

9. Food and Agriculture Organization of the United Nations. At the World Agricultural Forum, in St. Louis, Missouri.

Chapter 2

1. World Bank. Countries and Regions. www.worldbank.org/html/extdr/regions.htm, 2001.

2. World Bank. Developing countries—Population—2000. devdata.worldbank.org/external/dgsector.asp?rmdk=110&w=0&SMDK=500009, 2001.

3. World Bank. Twenty Questions About Poverty and Development. www.worldbank.org/poverty/quiz/whole.htm, 2001.

4. Lester R. Brown and others. *State of the World 2001* (New York: Worldwatch Institute, W.W. Norton & Son, 2001), p. 6.

5. Lester R. Brown and others, p. 6.

6. Dario Novellino. Indigenous Highlands in Transition: The Case of Ha Giang Province in Northern Vietnam. www.fao.org/DOCREP/003/X8050T/x8050t09.htm#P10 2222, accessed September 20, 2001.

7. Hernando de Soto. *The Mystery of Capital: Why Capitalism Triumphs in the West and Fails Everywhere Else* (New York: Basic Books, 2000), p. 33.

8. Mark S. Langevin and Peter Rosset. Land Reform From Below: The Landless Workers Movement in Brazil. MST Brazil. www.mstbrazil.org/rosset.html, accessed August 22, 2001.

9. Jason Mark. Brazil: Taking Back the Land. Greenleft Weekly, issue 437. www.greenleft.org.au/back/2001/437/437p20.htm, February 21, 2001.

10. Molly Moore. Desperate Farmers in Turkey Put Their Village Up For Sale. Washington Post. www.library.cornell.edu/colldev/mideast/calli.htm, May 15, 2001, p. A10.

11. Hernando de Soto. *The Constituency of Terror* (New York Times, October 15, 2001), p. A23.
12. Women for Women International. Celebrating Success. www.womenforwomen.org/success.htm, accessed November 30, 2001.

Chapter 3

1. World Bank. Twenty Questions About Poverty and Development. www.worldbank.org/poverty/quiz/whole.htm, 2001.
2. George McGovern. *The Third Freedom: Ending Hunger in Our Time* (New York: Simon & Schuster, 2001), p. 117.
3. Lester R. Brown. *Tough Choices: Facing the Challenge of Food Scarcity* (New York: Worldwatch Institute, W.W. Norton & Company, 1996), p. 27.
4. International Development Enterprises. India: Dangi Marandi. www.ideorg.org/whatsnew/testimonials/india-marandi.htm, accessed September 9, 2001.
5. Eric Kashambuzi. *The Paradox of Hunger and Abundance* (Orlando, FL: Rivercross Publishing, Inc., 1999), p. 79.

Chapter 4

1. George McGovern. *The Third Freedom: Ending Hunger in Our Time* (New York: Simon & Schuster, 2001), p. 11.
2. Lester R. Brown. *Tough Choices: Facing the Challenge of Food Scarcity* (New York: Worldwatch Institute, W.W. Norton & Company, 1996), p. 30.
3. Leslie Kaufman. Pakistanis Urge U.S. to Suspend Textile Tariffs. New York Times. www.ifai.com/NewsDetails.php?ID=1200, November 8, 2001, p. C5.
4. Zero Population Growth. The Demographic Facts of Life. www.zpg.org/Communications/demfacts.PDF, Fall 2001.
5. Nation by Nation. www.nationbynation.com/sweden, accessed February 14, 2002.
6. Lester R. Brown and others. *State of the World 2001* (New York: Worldwatch Institute, W.W. Norton & Son, 2001), p. 156.

Chapter 5

1. Ray Moseley. Iraq Is Draining Away 5,000-Year Way of Life. Chicago Tribune. www.kuwaitinfo.org/Home/current_issues/Iraq_Is_Draining_Away_500_Year_Way_of_Life/Iraq_is_draining-away-5.htm, May 22, 2001.
2. George McGovern. *The Third Freedom: Ending Hunger in Our Time* (New York: Simon & Schuster, 2001), p. 101.
3. Karl Vick. Death Toll in Congo War May Approach 3 Million. Washington Post. home.att.net/~drew.hamre/refw3congo.htm, April 30, 2001, p. A01.

Chapter 6

1. Peter K Eisinger. *Toward an End to Hunger in America* (Washington, D.C.: Brookings Institute Press, 1998), p. 2.
2. Eisinger, p. 24.
3. George McGovern. *The Third Freedom: Ending Hunger in Our Time* (New York: Simon & Schuster, 2001), p. 70.
4. Bread for the World. Hunger Basics. www.bread.org/hungerbasics/faq.html, accessed November 3, 2001.
5. Economic Research Service, U.S. Department of Agriculture. Food Security in the United States: Conditions and Trends. www.ers.usda.gov/briefing/foodsecurity/trends/index.htm, accessed September 30, 2001.
6. Bread For the World, Hunger Basics.
7. Bread For the World, Hunger Basics.

Chapter 7

1. George McGovern. *The Third Freedom: Ending Hunger in Our Time* (New York: Simon & Schuster, 2001), p. 117.

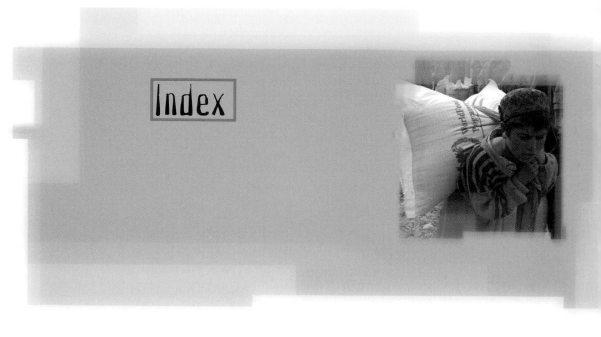

Index

Page numbers in *italics* refer to illustrations.